THE
DOG
BOOK

Dogs of Historical Distinction

Published in Great Britain in 2014 by Old House books & maps
c/o Osprey Publishing, PO Box 883, Oxford OX2 9PH, UK.
c/o Osprey Publishing, PO Box 3985, New York, NY 10185-3985, USA.
Website: www.oldhousebooks.co.uk

Kathleen Walker-Meikle has asserted her right under the Copyright, Designs and Patents Act, 1988, to be identified
as the author of this book.

Images are acknowledged as follows:
Ashmolean Museum, University of Oxford, UK / The Bridgeman Art Library, page 21; The Bridgeman Art Library,
pages 38, 49, 77; British Library Images, pages 15, 16, 17, 36, 43, 64, 114; British Library Creative Commons, pages
5, 35, 103, 108, 144; © The Trustees of the British Museum, pages 18 and 23; Chiesa del Sacro Cuore, Florence
/ The Bridgeman Art Library, page 24; De Agostini Picture Library / G. Dagli Orti / The Bridgeman Art Library,
pages 7, 8; Koninklijk Museum voor Schone Kunsten, Belgium / The Bridgeman Art Library, page 47; Lewis
Walpole Library, pages 58, 73, 85, 86, 90, 92, 93, 111, 132; Library of Congress, title page, pages 83, 98, 100-1,
109, 19; Louvre, Paris, France / The Bridgeman Art Library, page 13; Mary Evans Picture Library, pages 57, 89,
123-4, 138, 143; Musee Conde, France / The Bridgeman Art Library, page 41; Musee Crozatier, Le Puy-en-Velay
/ The Bridgeman Art Library, page 69; Musee de la Tapisserie, Bayeux, France / With special authorisation of the
city of Bayeux / The Bridgeman Art Library, page 25; Musee de la Ville de Paris, Musee du Petit-Palais, France /
The Bridgeman Art Library, page 113; Nostell Priory, Yorkshire, UK / National Trust Photographic Library / John
Hammond / The Bridgeman Art Library, page 53; Private Collection / © Arthur Ackermann Ltd., London / The
Bridgeman Art Library, cover image; Pushkin Museum, Moscow, Russia / Giraudon / The Bridgeman Art Library,
page 74; The Royal Collection © 2014 Her Majesty Queen Elizabeth II / The Bridgeman Art Library, pages 66, 94,
107; Schloss Sanssouci, Germany / The Bridgeman Art Library, page 79; Topfoto.co.uk, pages 126, 131 and 141;
Victoria & Albert Museum, London, UK / The Bridgeman Art Library, page 30; Wellcome Collection Images, pages
10, 29, 33, 50, 55, 63, 80-1, 96, and 119.

Printed in China through World Print Ltd.
14 15 16 17 18   10 9 8 7 6 5 4 3 2 1

THE
DOG BOOK

Dogs of Historical Distinction

Kathleen Walker-Meikle

• OLD HOUSE •

INTRODUCTION

Dogs have been man's closest companion for over 10,000 years, ever since they were first domesticated from the grey wolf. Since then, *Canis lupus familiaris* can be traced nearly all over the globe, in breeds from the burly Newfoundland to the diminutive Pekingese. Over the millennia, they have been keen hunters, trusted guardians or beloved pets; but some of the dogs featured in this book had more a unusual place in society, such as the multitude of performing dogs who delighted audiences on the stage and, later, on the screen. Wherever their owners went, dogs followed, and so we also find dogs in the middle of battlefields (occasionally getting lost!), in witchcraft trials, mascots for regiments and postal workers, and even flying over the North Pole…

Throughout history, the most praised quality of the dog – and that which set it apart from other animals – has been its loyalty and devotion to its master or mistress. Although this is an anthropomorphic interpretation of canine behaviour, it forms the basis of many of the tales found in this book, such as those animals pining on their master's grave, or trying to save them from danger. Basic rituals of dog-ownership – such as keeping the animal fed, or adorning it with specialist accessories such as collars and leashes – are also in evidence across the ages, along with the related perils of overfeeding your pet or extravagantly spending a fortune on coats (or in the case of one Indian prince, an elaborate canine wedding complete with elephants in attendance!).

This book can only recount a fraction of famous accounts of historical dogs, but presents a selection of memorable movie-stars, pampered palace pets, performing poodles and dogs on the battlefield through various mediums including satirical poems and anxious newspaper notices for stolen animals. There are loyal dogs and spoiled pets, tales of exemplary behaviour and misbehaviour, and the beloved companions of famous figures including Prince Rupert of the Rhine, Lord Byron and President Roosevelt. In literature they have been alternately praised and satirised, due to the vast affection their owners have long lavished upon them. From Roman mosaics to the Bayeux Tapestry and depictions of the Last Supper, the iconography of dogs can also be found almost everywhere, and touching personal portraits of owners and their dogs reveal how a pet often became an essential and proud part of their identity. Keep an eye on history, and you will start seeing dogs everywhere!

Kathleen Walker-Meikle

An inscribed limestone tablet discovered at Giza in 1935 attests the elaborate burial of Abuwtiyuw, most likely an *Ancient Egyptian sighthound,* which belonged to an unknown pharaoh of the Sixth Dynasty (2345–2181 BC). Only the tablet survives, but it is likely that the dog was mummified, judging from the gift of linen. It reads:

The dog which was the guard of His Majesty, Abuwtiyuw is his name. His Majesty ordered that he be buried [ceremonially], that he be given a coffin from the royal treasury, fine linen in great quantity, [and] incense. His Majesty [also] gave perfumed ointment, and [ordered] that a tomb be built for him by the gangs of masons. His Majesty did this for him in order that he [the dog] might be Honoured [before the great god, Anubis]

Dog mummies have been discovered in many Egyptian sites; the largest collection of ancient canine graves is the burial ground of several hundred unearthed at Ashkelon (in modern day Israel). The dogs were buried there over eight decades in the second half of the fifth century BC. They were all sighthounds (resembling modern greyhounds or whippets), the most documented of Egyptian dog breeds.

Relief of a scene at Necropolis, featuring two Ancient Egyptian sighthounds (c.2349 BC).

Homer's *Odyssey*, written around 800 BC, recounts the legendary Greek hero Odysseus's long adventures to return home to his kingdom of Ithaca after the end of the Trojan War.

Odysseus' faithful dog *Argos* had been a young puppy when his master left for war, and is the only one on Ithaca to recognise him when he returns after twenty years. Neglected and covered in fleas, Argos lay on a dung heap by the stables, but pricked up his ears at his master's approach, wagging his tail. Odysseus saw Argos but could not greet him, due to being in disguise – instead he shed a hidden tear for the loyal hound. He asked his companion, the swineherd Eumaus, about the dog. He explained that the dog belonged to someone who had died in a far country and had been a magnificent hunting hound but had now fallen on evil times, for his master was gone and the women no longer took care of him. Odysseus entered the hall of the palace and faithful Argos passed into the darkness of death after seeing his master once more.

This detail from a seventeenth-century tapestry shows Argos recognising his master Ulysses.

The *Egyptian god Anubis* oversaw the mummification process. By weighing the heart of the deceased against the feather of truth, he decided whether they should enter the otherworld or be eaten by the Devourer (part lion, hippopotamus and crocodile).

Anubis is his name in Greek – his Egyptian names are Anpu, Inpw and Yinupu. He had many epithets, such as 'He Who is in the Mummy-Wrappings' and 'Chief of the Necropolis'. He is depicted as half-human jackal, although there is confusion concerning exactly which canid he was supposed to be – a jackal, a wolf or even a wild dog. Recent DNA studies have proved that the Egyptian jackal is actually a subspecies of the grey wolf.

In Egypt, his cult centred in a town the Greeks called Cynopolis, meaning the 'City of the Dogs'. The Greek writer Plutarch (c. AD 46–120) wrote that a small civil war erupted when a resident of Cynopolis ate an Oxyrhynchos fish. The people of Oxyrhynchos began to attack dogs, which resulted in communal violence. The cult of Anubis was still extant in the second century AD.

———————◆×———————

Glazed ceramic amulet representing Anubis, the guardian of the tombs.
Dated 4000–30 BC.

11

An association between *dogs and the afterlife* appears
in many cultures.

In Greek mythology, Cerberus is the fearsome multi-headed dog
guarding the entrance to the underworld. In Virgil's *Aeneid,* Aeneas'
sneaks past Cerberus after his guide, the Sibyl, throws him drugged
honey-cakes. Cerberus is also lulled to sleep when the musician Orpheus
comes in search of his wife Eurydice, and when the god Hermes gives
him water from the river Lethe, which brings forgetfulness. Capturing
Cerberus and bringing him to King Eurystheus is the last labour of Greek
hero Hercules. Hades, god of the underworld, gives his permission on
the condition that the dog is unharmed. Hercules overpowers the beast
and presents him to Eurystheus, who hides in terror when he sees the
dog. Hercules then returns Cerberus to his home.

In *Norse mythology,* Garm is the terrifying hound that stands by the
gate of Hell. The poem Grímnismál in the Poetic Edda recounts that
he is the best of dogs. In *Welsh mythology,* the Cŵn Annwn (dogs of
Annwn) guard the otherworld.

An Ionian Hydria depicting Heracles bringing Cerberus to Eurystheus, c.530 BC.

Sirius is the brightest star (actually a binary star system) in the sky. It is part of the constellation Canis Major (Greater Dog), who is supposed to have been the faithful hound of the hunter Orion, and is also known as *the 'Dog Star'* or Canicula. Associated with them both is the constellation Canis Minor (Little Dog), whose brightest star is Procyon ('Before the dog').

The 'Dog Days' (*dies caniculares* in Latin) are the hot days of summer, and began when Sirius was seen just before, or at the same time as, sunrise (this does not happen now due to the precession of equinoxes). The 'Dog Days' of July and August were associated with rabid dogs and fevers and other diseases, as Homer recounts in the *Iliad*:

> *Sirius rises late in the dark, liquid sky*
> *On summer nights, star of stars,*
> *Orion's Dog they call it, brightest*
> *Of all, but an evil portent, bringing heat*
> *And fevers to suffering humanity.*

———◆———

A ninth-century representation of the constellation Canis Major. Sirius is the bright shining gold star on the dog's tongue.

Namquepedes subter rutilo cumlumine clare
ferundus ille canis stellarum lucere fulgens
Hunc tegit obscurus subter praecordia uesper
Et uero toto spumis decorpore flammam
Aestifero saulidis erumpit flatibus ignes
Totus ab ore micans ticitur mortalibus ardor
His ubi se pariter cum sole inlumina caeli
Exulit haud patitur foliorum tegmine frustra
Suspensos animos arbusta ornata tenere
Nam quorum stirpis tellus amplexa prehendit
Hec augens aninguitali flamina mulcet
Asquorum nequeunt radices findere terras
Denudat folus ramos et cortice truncos

SYRIUS

Relief from the Kerameikos necropolis in Athens, depicting a fight between a dog and a cat (510 BC).

Mosaic representing a guard dog, from Pompeii in the first century AD.

A moving marble tombstone, now in the British Museum, was erected for a beloved dog called Margarita (Latin for pearl) in the second century AD:

Gaul was my birthplace. The oyster from the rich water's waves gave me a name suited to my beauty. I learned to run boldly through treacherous woods and to pursue shaggy beasts in the hills. Heavy chains never restrained me, nor did my snow-white body ever suffer any blows. I used to lie in my master's and mistress's soft laps, and curl up on their bed when I was tired. I used to talk more than I should, with my dog's dumb mouth, though no-one feared my barking. But alas, misfortune befell me when whelping, and now this little marble slab marks where the earth enfolds me.

Marble statue of two playful dogs, first or second century AD, known as 'the Townley Greyhounds'.

There were many *types of dog in the Classical world.* The two most popular breeds for hunting and guard duties were the Spartan dog and the Molossian dog. The former was a lean hound best suited 'for the swift chase of gazelle and deer' while the Molossian was large with a short muzzle, good for attacking bulls and boars. Others were the vertragi from Gaul and the shaggy Agassean hound, an export from Britain.

The favourite lapdog was the Melitaean, which probably originated in Malta. They were small, with long hair and short legs. A traditional belief claimed that if they were pressed to the stomach, they alleviated the symptoms of stomach-ache.

There were also *performing dogs in Ancient Rome,* such as the one who performed at the Theatre of Marcellus before the Emperor Vespasian. The act consisted of giving the dog food that the audience believed was poisoned. The dog then began to shiver and shake, stagger around and collapse. The actors moved it about to give the impression that the dog was dead. But then, on a cue, the dog 'woke' up, raised its head and ran to the actors.

Detail of a cup featuring a Laconian hound scratching his head, c.500 BC.

The first-century Roman poet Martial wrote an epigram on a very beloved little dog:

…Issa is the darling little puppy of Publius.
If she whines, you will think that she speaks;
She feels sorrow and joy.
She sleeps resting on his neck, and takes her naps
Such that no breaths are heard;
And compelled by the desire of her bladder,
Not a single drop has befouled the coverlet,
But she awakens him with a caressing paw, and advises
That she be put down from the couch, and asks to be picked up.
There is such great modesty in the little puppy;
She does not know Venus, nor do we find
A mate worthy of such a delicate girl.
So that her last day does not snatch her away entirely,
Publius is portraying her on a painted tablet…

———◆———

Terracotta figure of a rather rotund pet dog, first century AD, Campania.

A large dog gnaws on a bone by Judas' feet in James van der Straet's sixteenth-century fresco of the Last Supper. A cat can also be seen, cowering behind a stool.

This detail from the eleventh-century Bayeux Tapestry shows William, Duke of Normandy, taking Harold to his palace at Rouen, accompanied by two hounds.

Canine loyalty to their owners has been a popular and enduring theme throughout history. The Roman author Pliny the Elder recounted in his *Natural History* (first century AD) how the captured king of the Garamentes in North Africa was rescued when his many dogs attacked his captors. Another of Pliny's accounts tells of an executed man who was thrown into the Tiber; his faithful dog leapt into the river and tried to rescue the corpse.

A popular medieval French tale recounts that when a man named Aubry de Montdidier was murdered by a man called Macaire, the victim's dog showed such hatred of the murderer that a duel was arranged between them. The dog won the trial by combat and the murderer confessed and was hanged.

The Norse *Hakon the Good's Saga*, written in the early thirteenth century, tells the story of *Saurr the Dog King*. When King Eysteinn of Oppland conquered Trondheim (both in modern Norway) he sent Onund, his son, to be their king. The locals soon killed Onund, and Eysteinn then gave them a choice of either his slave or his dog to be their next king. They chose the dog, called Saurr, who 'ruled' for three years. He had a gold collar, a throne, a palace, and courtiers, and signed documents with his paw-print. Dog-kings are not unusual in medieval Scandinavian literature. In his *Deeds of the Danes*, the author Saxo Grammaticus recounts of a Swedish warrior called Gunnar who invaded Norway and appointed a dog as their ruler to shame them. Governors ruled in the name of the dog, and courtiers had to take care of it. Anyone who did not show the dog respect was mutilated.

A political cartoon on George III, titled 'Father Peters leading his mangy whelp to be touched for the evil' (1780).

Hold out my Sons to the End & I'll give you a Crown of Glory,
He cocks his Tail yet.

In the Arthurian tales of *Tristan and Isolde*, the couples' dogs play a major part. In Gottfried von Strassburg's version of the legend, Tristan fights a giant to get a little multi-coloured, long-haired lapdog as a gift for Isolde. The dog, named *Petitcreiu,* is a *Feehündchen* (fairy lap dog) from Avalon, who wears a collar with a magical bell that banishes the sadness of the owner. Petitcreiu does not bark, eat, or drink, but is a cheerful canine companion to his new mistress. Isolde has a little kennel made of gold and precious stones, with a brocade bed. But, not wishing to be happy without her lover, Isolde removes the bell – thus turning Petitcreiu into an ordinary pet dog.

When the adulterous couple attempt to avoid detection as they hide in a grotto, Tristan trains his hound Huidan to hunt in silence, and not bark at game. In the Middle English version, *Sir Tristem*, Huiden accidently licks the cup with the love potion that the lovers drink: 'they loved with all their might. And Hodain did also'.

Stained glass image referencing The Book of Tobit, depicting Tobias and Sara on their wedding night (c.1520). Tobias' dog, asleep on their bed, is the only positive representation of a dog in the Bible.

Most medieval dogs were fed bread, and 'bread for dogs' is a common entry in household accounts. However, the dogs of the wealthy might enjoy more extravagant meals. In Geoffrey Chaucer's *The Canterbury Tales*, the elegant Prioress is described thus:

She had some little dogs, that she fed
On roasted flesh, or milk and fine white bread.

Nevertheless, spoiling pet dogs with high quality food was frowned upon by some. John Bromyard, an English Dominican in the fourteenth century, complained:

The wealthy provide for their dogs more readily than for the poor, more abundantly and more delicately too; so that, whereas the poor are so famished that they would greedily devour bran-bread, dogs turn up their noses at the sight of wafer-bread, and spurn what is offered to them, trampling it under their feet. They **must be offered the daintiest flesh,** *the first and choicest portion of every dish. If full, they refuse it. Then there is wailing about them, as though they were ill.*

Detail from a print depicting the interior of an apothecary's shop, 1568.

The fourteenth-century Italian scholar Francisco Petrarch was very fond of dogs, and they appear throughout his correspondence as models of affection. He wrote that the elements of a simple life were 'clothes to wear, servants, a horse to ride, a roof and a bed, and *a dog for company*'. One of his dogs was a gift sent from his patron, Cardinal Giovanni Colonna, as a 'companion and source of comfort'. In 1347 he described how the dog was settling into his new home in Vaucluse. The dog became accustomed to a simpler life: eating bread and water; living in a small house; running around the countryside and swimming. This exercise apparently cured the dog of mange, which Petrarch claimed was due to the unhealthy airs of Avignon.

The dog was a perfect companion for the scholar, thoughtfully chasing away any villagers who turned up to annoy Petrarch with their petty troubles and informing his master if he had slept too long by whimpering and scratching at the door. Although the dog was prone to barking at strangers, he would be very friendly towards Petrarch's friends, with dropped ears and a cheerful wagging tail.

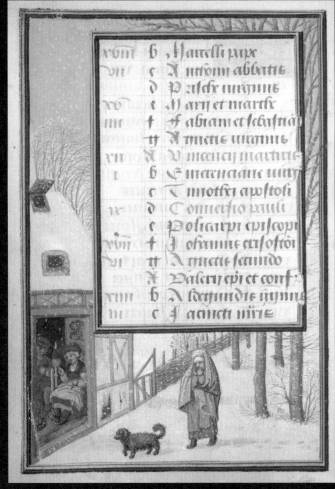

xviii	b	Marcelli pape
vii	c	Antonii abbatis
	d	Prische uirginis
xvi	e	Marii et marthe
v	f	fabiani et sebastiani
	g	Agnetis uirginis
xiii	A	Vincencii martiris
ii	b	Emerenciane uirginis
	c	Timothei apostoli
x	d	Conuersio pauli
	e	Policarpi episcopi
xviii	f	Johannis crisostomi
vi	g	Agnetis secundo
	A	Valerii epi et conf
xiii	b	Aldegundis uirginis
iii	c	Sancti nitie

Johannes rex genuit videlicet

The Master of Game, a *medieval hunting treatise* written by Edward, Duke of York (d. 1415) lists raches (scent hounds), greyhounds, alaunts, mastiffs, and terriers as suitable hunting dogs. They all had different duties. For example, a lymer (bloodhound) on a leash would find the game before the pack arrived, the raches would run the quarry down while the greyhounds would only be released near the end of the hunt. Hunting was a very ritualised activity in the Middle Ages and a stag hunt with hounds would end with the curée, when the dogs were rewarded with meat from the deer's carcass.

One manuscript of *The Master of Game* has a list of over a thousand suitable dog names including Troy, Blawnche, Nosewise, Swepestake, Smylfeste, Trynket, Amiable, Nameles, Clenche, Bragge, Holdfast, Crab, Ringwood and Absolom. Manuscripts of Gaston Phébus's *Livre de la Chasse* suggest Bauderon, Baudellette, Bloquiau, Briffault, Cliquau, Fillette, Huielle, Huiiau, Loquebaut, Mirre and Ostine among many others as names for hounds.

A fourteenth-century miniature of King John hunting a stag with his hounds.

Royal dogs could be very well cared for. When his royal master was deposed, Richard II's greyhound Math abandoned his master and ran to meet the new king, Henry IV. Henry saw this as a good omen - particularly as the greyhound was one of his symbols - and he even let Math sleep on his bed. An entry in the accounts of Henry VIII lists a man called Robin who was paid for using 'a hair-cloth to rub the dogges with'.

Before leaving for the fatal battle of Mohács in 1526, King Louis II of Hungary cried out: 'Take good care of the little dogs! And wash them twice a week!'

Detail from Titian's 'Venus of Urbino' (1538).

Many medieval texts reveal *medical treatments for dogs*. One ointment for *mange* (given in *The Master of Game*) consists of honey, verdigris, nut oil, water and valerian leaf. For treating *'sickness in the hound's ears'*, the author recommended washing the ear with luke-warm wine four times a day, followed by oil and milk infused with chamomile, while taking care that the dog did not scratch.

The thirteenth-century scholar Albertus Magnus wrote that dogs suffering from *scabies* should be bled, and the spots anointed with an ointment of mercury, sulphur, neetle seeds and butter. *Spines in the paws* should be drawn out with a mixture of bran and lard. If a dog grew *too thin* it should be fed with copious quantities of butter, and *fleas* could be removed by covering the dog with olive oil. He also recommended porridge, soft bread and whey for overweight pet dogs as 'they almost always die of constipation'.

Rabies was greatly feared, and a common prophylactic was to cut the 'worm' (the mucous membrane) under a dog's tongue. The French surgeon Henri de Mondeville suggested sea-bathing: 'I have often seen people and animals taken to the seashore who already exhibit the bad signs, at peace and docile as they are led.'

'Caring for the Hounds', from Gaston Phébus's Livre de la Chasse (fifteenth century).

St Roch is the *patron saint of dogs*, and of plague. The saint's hagiographies recount that he grew ill in the early fourteenth century, after carrying for the sick in Piacenza. Thrown out of the town, he wandered around a nearby forest in great hunger, where he met a dog with a loaf of bread. The dog presented him with the bread and licked his buboes (swellings caused by the plague). The dog's owner, a nobleman called Gothard, noticed that his dog was coming every day to the dinner table, removing a loaf of bread and then leaving the hall. After following the dog to the forest and seeing St Roch eating the bread, Gothard took him in and cared for him. The cult of St Roch is spread through the world. In Bolivia his feast day (16 August) is celebrated as the special day for dogs, who are decked out in coloured ribbons and given treats and great affection.

Similarly, the thirteenth-century Carmelite saint Simon Stock was fed by his own small dog (who brought pieces of bread for his master) when he lived in a forest in Kent.

The thirteenth-century preacher Étienne de Bourbon discovered that women in the diocese of Lyons were taking their children to a forest shrine dedicated to a *'Saint Guinefort'*, protector of children. To his horror, he discovered that Guinefort was a dog, to whom the locals prayed to when ill or in need. The story went that a knight and his lady had left their baby alone in the house, and a giant serpent had approached the cradle. It was attacked by Guinefort, the family's greyhound, and the cradle was knocked over during the fight. When the knight returned to find the cradle empty and the dog's jaws covered in blood, he assumed that Guinefort had murdered the baby. Only after killing his dog did he discover the baby safely asleep and the remains of the dead snake. Grieving, they buried the dog and planted trees besides the grave, which later became the shrine. The cult of Guinefort survived until the early twentieth century.

A similar story appears in Welsh folklore, although the man is Llywelyn the Great, Prince of Gwynedd, the hound is called Gelert and the attacker is a wolf rather than a snake. The basic theme of the story (owner murdering loyal pet) is very old, and first found in the Sanskrit Panchatantra (the pet is a mongoose).

An inventory of the French king Charles V in 1380 lists very *ornate and expensive dog collars* for both pet dogs and hunting hounds. They include 'one silver collar with bells for a little dog' and 'very small collar made with blue cloth adorned with gold fleur de lys and three little gold bells, secured by a gold buckle', and 'thirteen collars for greyhounds and other dogs decorated with silver'. In the fifteenth century, Louis XI's greyhound Cherami had a scarlet velvet collar decorated with twenty pearls and eleven rubies.

In England, Henry VIII's inventories feature 'two greyhound collars of crimson velvet and cloth of gold, with locking spikes', 'one collar of white velvet, embroidered with pearls and silver' and a 'collar embroidered with pomegranates and roses with turrets of silver and gilt', which would have been for one of Catherine of Aragon's dogs (the pomegranate and the turrets of Castile being her symbols). The collars identified the dogs as royal – which would have been helpful for Cut and Ball, two of Henry's dogs who were always getting lost.

Detail from the Seven Sacraments Altarpiece (c.1445), showing a woman reading with a small dog.

In *sixteenth-century Italy*, Isabella d'Este, Marquise of Mantua, was very attached to her pet dogs. The author Mateo Bandello remarked that when 'the sound of little dogs barking was heard' in any rooms of the palace, it was 'a sign that madama [Isabella] was coming in'. Her most beloved was a little dog called Aura, who accompanied her everywhere. When Aura died in an accident, Isabella could not be consoled. She arranged for the dog to be buried in a lead casket in an elaborate tomb, and read out dozens of Latin poems that were written all over Italy in Aura's honour.

Her son Federico Gonzaga, Duke of Mantua, was equally devoted to small dogs. In 1511, one of the puppies from his mother's dog Fanina was reserved for Federico, and named Zaphyro. The dog was described as a 'bel cagnolo' (beautiful little dog), 'the most loveliest and appealing in the world', of a reddish colour, with patches of white around the neck, tail and feet.

This portrait of Federico Gonzaga by Titian, completed in 1529, features one of his small dogs. It is a rarity in sixteenth-century portraiture, in which men are usually accompanied by large dogs rather than lapdogs.

The late sixteenth-century Belgian *scholar Justus Lipsius* adored his dogs, whom he named Melissa, Saphyrus, Mopsulus and Mopsus, *and took a dog with him* when lecturing at the University of Louvain.

He wrote poems extolling their virtues. In one, Saphyrus was described a charming rather ancient little Dutch dog of thirteen years with white fur and a brown head and ears, and the 'jewel of all dogs in Belgium', charming and beautiful. Mopsulus, a two-year-old snub-nosed dog, had a white body and a red muzzle speckled with white. Mopsulus had a cunning and snappish temperament. A poem written from the point of view of Mopsulus has the little dog recount how he sleeps on his master's bed and is the master's master (*domini dominus*). Mopsus, a three-year-old chestnut dog from Scotland, had chestnut fur scattered with white spots.

When Saphyrus died at the grand age of fifteen, Lipsius wrote an elegy praising the dog who would wag his tail, bounce and bark, demand attention, and amuse his master with tricks. Lipsius concluded by asking for Cerberus to be kind to his dog in the underworld.

An alchemist in his study, attended by his dog (wood engraving).

Lady Lisle, the wife of the deputy of Calais, owned a small dog called Purkoy, whose name came from the French 'Pourquoi' ('why?') due to its inquisitive expression. However, when told that the new English queen Anne Boleyn wanted the dog, she reluctantly bowed to pressure and gave him up. John Husse, a member of the king's household, wrote to her in January 1534 to insist: 'There is no remedy, your ladyship must needs depart with your little Purquoy, the which I know well shall grieve your ladyship not a little.'

Purkoy arrived in the queen's household soon after, and Sir Francis Bryan wrote to Lord Lisle and told him to thank his wife for sending 'her little dog, which was so proper and so well liked by the Queen that it remained not above an hour in my hands but that her Grace took it from me'. When *Anne Boleyn's beloved little Purkoy* died from a fall, fearing the queen's grief, no one dared to inform her of the dog's misfortune. It was left to Henry VIII to break the sad news.

Portrait of Sir Thomas More and his Family, after a painting by Hans Holbein the Younger (dated 1590s).

Anna Crisacria Joannes
Mori Sponsa anno · 15.

Joannes Morus pater
anno · 76.

Thomas Morus an
no · 50.

Joannes Morus Thoma
Filius anno · 19.

henricus Pattison
Thoma seruus.

Cecilia Heroud Thoma Mori
filia anno · 20.

Margareta Ropera Thoma Mori
filia anno · 22.

In 1570 John Caius, physician and one of the founders of Gonville and Caius College, wrote *De canibus Britannicis* (translated as *On English Dogges*).

In it, he described hunting dogs (including harriers, terriers, bloodhounds, gazehounds, greyhounds, lymers, tumblers and the 'thieving dog') and fowling dogs (spaniels, setters, water spaniels and the 'fisher'). He then discussed companion dogs, in particular 'the delicate, neat, and pretty kind of dog called the Spaniel gentle or the comforter' which is a 'pleasant playfellow'.

For working dogs, he listed mastiffs, the 'dog keeper' (a guard dog), butcher's dogs, the now extinct Molossus, dog messengers (that 'carries letters from place to place, wrapped up cunningly in his leather collar'), mooners (dogs that bark at the moon), tinker's curs (that carried the tinker's buckets on their backs), and 'defending' dogs. Caius finished his treatise with dogs 'of mongrel and rascal sort', including the warner (which just barked), the turnspit (turned spits in kitchens) and the 'dancer' (a performing dog).

Illustrations from Conrad Gesner's Icones animalium quadrupedum (1560).

CANIS ſagax ſanguinarius, apud Anglos.

ANGLICE A Bludhunde. Eadem hujus natura videtur, quæ Canis Scotici furum deprehenſoris, proximè deſcripti.

CANIS Auiarius Campeſtris, quo Falconarij (id eſt, qui cum Accipitribus aucupantur) ad Perdicum aut Phaſianorum ferè aucupiũ utuntur. Sunt hujus generis omnis ferè coloris (inquit Caius) ſed magna ex parte candidi: & ſi quas maculas habeant, rubræ ſunt, raræ & majores. Peculiare nomen Anglis non habet, niſi ab ave, ad cujus venationem natura eſt propenſior.

GERMANICE Ein Vogelhund/ wirdt zu den fåderſpil gebraucht/ Råbhůner oder Phaſanen/ ꝛc. zu fangen.

CANIS Aviarius aquaticus. Qui per aquas venatur (inquit Caius) propenſione naturali, accedente mediocri documento, major his (aviarius qui in ſicco venantur) eſt, & promiſſo pilo naturaliter per totum corpus. Ego tamen ab armis ad poſteriores ſuffragines atque extremam caudam depinxi detõſum, vt vſus noſter poſtulat, quò pilis nudus expeditior ſit, & minùs per natationes retardetur.

ANGLICE A Waterſpaguelle.

The *Anglo-Saxon Chronicle* tells of huge black dogs in a demonic hunt around Peterborough in the early twelfth century, and a *demonic black dog* (usually called Black Shuck) appears repeatedly in English folklore. On 4 August 1577, the dog was seen in two churches in Suffolk. In Blythburgh it raced through the nave, killed people, caused the steeple to fall down and left scorch marks on the door (still displayed to this day). Abraham Fleming wrote that it also killed congregants at Bungay, 'running all along down the body of the church with great swiftness.'

Heinrich Cornelius Agrippa (1486-1535), author of various magical and astrological treatises, kept two dogs, a black male called Monsieur and a bitch called Mamselle. Agrippa allowed Monsieur to eat beside him and sleep on his bed, provoking many contemporaries and later commentators to believe the dog was in fact a familiar demon. The black dog resurfaces in the Faust legends as *the Devil in disguise*. In Johann Wolfgang von Goethe's play 'Faust', Mephistopheles is first seen by Faust in the guise of a black poodle (*schwarze Püdel*).

A woodcut of Faust performing magic, with the Devil in the shape of a black dog, accompanied by dancing witches and hell-fire.

O, tis a foul thing, when a cur cannot keep himself in all
companies. I would have, as one should say, one that
takes upon him to be a Dog indeed, to

LAUNCE
Teaching his Dog crab
to behave as a Dog

bad more wit th
that he did, I th
fort sure as I liv

The 'rascally sort' mentioned by Caius is exemplified by Crab, the only dog playing a *part in a Shakespeare play*. In 'Two Gentlemen of Verona', Proteus's servant Launce appears with the stage direction 'Enter Launce, with his Dog'.

Launce's affection for Crab is rather one-sided. As the entire household except Crab wept with news of his departure, he comments: 'I think Crab, my dog, be the sourest-natured dog that lives'.

Crab was not the only role available for a canine actor on the Elizabethan stage. Among many others, Ben Jonson's 'Everyman out of His Humour' (1599) has the stage direction 'Enter Puntarvolo and Carlo, followed by serving-men, one leading a dog, the other bearing a bag' and 'Histriomastix' by John Marston (1599) has the direction 'Enter Velure and Lyon-rash, with a water-spaniel and a duck'.

James I of England loved hunting and hounds. He even called his principal secretary Sir Robert Cecil *'my little beagle'*. In 1613 he flew into a rage on hearing that his 'most special and principal hound', Jewel, had been shot in the hunting field. He was mollified when he heard that his own queen, Anne of Denmark, had accidentally shot the dog when aiming for a deer. He even gave her a diamond worth £2,000 as a 'legacy from his dead dog'.

In 1615, the king heard a debate on 'whether dogs could make syllogisms', at Cambridge. John Preston of Queens' College claimed that a hound reasoned 'in his mind', for example, 'The hare is gone either this way or that way; smells out the minor with his nose, namely, She is not gone this way; and follows the conclusion, Ergo this way, with open mouth'.

Matthew Wren of Pembroke College argued that they determined the path by smell alone. The King took Preston's side, arguing with an example of one of his own dog's actions. The moderator diplomatically suggested that perhaps royal dogs are exceptional, unlike common hounds.

James I's descendants inherited his love for dogs.

In 1606 his son Henry, Prince of Wales, sent a pack of dogs to Louis, the French dauphin (later Louis XIII) 'in whole-hearted and firm friendship'. At Henry's early death, his brother Charles succeeded as Prince of Wales, and later as King Charles I. He began the *Stuart association with spaniels*, and took his beloved spaniel Rogue with him to Carisbrooke Castle during the Civil War. The dog stayed with the king until his execution in 1649.

In 1682, Charles' son James, Duke of York was the object of scurrilous rumour which alleged that when his ship the Gloucester went down, he abandoned the crew and jumped into small boat crying out *'Save the dogs'* and, after a short pause, '... and Colonel Churchill!' (the future Duke of Marlborough). Another version of the libel alleged that the Duke had abandoned even the dogs, and that his beloved dog Mumper had to tussle desperately with Sir Charles Scarborough, royal physician, for the last remaining plank. Both parties survived.

Dogs appear in the records of witch trials, usually as the *witch's familiar* or as demonic agent, such as the two dogs killed during the Salem witch trials.

In Essex in 1645, the Witchfinder Matthew Hopkins claimed that Elizabeth Clark had many animal familiars, including two dog-like familiars called Jamara, 'a fat spaniel without any legs at all, she said she kept him fat' and Vinegar Tom, a 'long-legg'd Greyhound, with an head like an Ox'. At the trial, in which twenty-three women stood accused, Helen Clark confessed that the Devil had appeared in her house in the likeness of a white dog, which she named Elimanzer and 'often fed him with milk-pottage'.

At the Pendle witch trials in 1612, Alice Device confessed that a 'thing like unto a black dog' appeared to her while she was out walking. It spoke English and asked her for her soul; in return he would give her the power to do anything she wanted. Alice's nine-year-old sister Jennet was the main witness for the prosecution and testified that her mother Elizabeth also had a familiar in the shape of a brown dog called Ball, and that her brother had conjured up a black dog to assist him in the murder of Anne Townley. All three were hanged for witchcraft.

whole name is Puddle, and Tobies Dog

VVhereunto is added the Challeng
which Prince *Griffins* Dogg called *Towzer*,
hath sent to Prince *Ruperts* Dogg *Puddle*, in
the behalfe of honest Pepper *Tobies* Dog.

Moreover the said Prince *Griffin* is newly gone to Oxford to lay the
wager, and to make up the M A T C H.

To him pudel.

Bite him pepper

Cavileer Dog

Roundhead cure

feb: 23   Printed at London for *I. Smith*, 1643.   1642

Prince Rupert of the Rhine, commander of the Royalist cavalry during the *English Civil War*, owned a large white poodle called *Boye*.

In 1642 the Royalist satirist John Cleveland wrote 'To Prince Rupert' in which he used the dog to mock their Parliamentarian opponents. He summoned the dog to the House of Commons, where Boye barked at the MPs and wagged his tail in sympathy with the High Church (he also humorously claimed that Boye would cock his leg whenever he heard the name John Pym, a leading Parliamentarian).

Another Royalist pamphlet has the Royalist dog 'Puddle' trading insults with 'Pepper', a Parliamentarian dog (who calls Boye a 'shag haired Cavalier's Dogge'). 'Puddle' claims that he prefers the aristocrats on the king's side to Pepper's 'red-cotton' soldiers. Pepper is so convinced that he swears to abjure roundheads and Puddle fetches sheep's wool for the converted Pepper's periwig.

Boye sadly died at the battle of Marston Moor in 1644. Despite being tied up for safety in the Royalist camp, Boye escaped and chased after his master, and was killed during the melee.

Few monarchs are associated with dogs as strongly as *Charles II*. The dogs slept in his rooms, while his wife Catherine of Braganza had a 'room where the Queen's dogs are kept' at Whitehall. They caused damage, and in 1683 he ordered a 'screen of wire, with the frame of walnut tree suitable to chairs, for his Majesty's new Bedchamber to preserve the bed from being spoiled by dogs'. The Earl of Ailesbury, as a Gentleman of the Bedchamber, remembered that he had to suffer the constant sounds of chiming clocks and the visits of a dozen dogs coming to the bed placed near the king.

The dogs were present at Council meetings and Samuel Pepys scoffed at the '*silliness of the King, playing with his dog* all the while, or his codpiece, and not minding the business'. On the king's death in 1685, John Evelyn wrote in diary how Charles had enjoyed 'having a number of little spaniels follow him and lie in the bedchamber, where he often suffered the bitches to puppy and give suck, which rendered it very offensive, and indeed made the whole court nasty and stinky.'

Detail from Sir Anthony van Dyck's portrait of the future Charles II and his siblings, already hinting at his early affection for dogs.

Dogs – even royal dogs – were regularly stolen. In a 1660 issue of the *Mercurius Publicus*, a royal advertisement announced:

We must call upon you again for a Black Dog between a greyhound and a spaniel, no white about him, only a streak on his breast, and his tail a little bobbed. It is His Majesties own Dog, and doubtless was stolen, for the dog was not born nor bred in England, and would never forsake His master. Whosoever finds him may acquaint any at Whitehall for the Dog was better known at Court, than those who stole him. Will they never leave robbing his Majesty!

Dog theft seemed to be endemic, as Charles II's mistress, the Duchess of Portsmouth advertised in the London Gazette in 1683 for the return of a 'young little black bitch' and offered two guineas to whoever would 'bring her to the porter at Whitehall Gate'; his uncle, Prince Rupert also advertised in 1677 when he lost a 'young white spaniel about six months old, with a black head, red eyebrows, and a black spot on his back… If anyone can bring him to Prince Rupert's Lodgings in the Stone Gallery at Whitehall he will be well rewarded for his pains'.

Detail from 'Church Interior' by Emanuel de Witte (seventeenth century).

However, perhaps even Charles II's affection for dogs pales in comparison with that of the French king *Henri III* (1551-1589). His small lapdogs were mostly 'petits chiens de Lyon' ('little lion dogs', resembling a modern bichon) and small spaniels. He received ambassadors with a red satin basket tied to his neck by a ribbon, in which several little dogs sat.

Henri spent more than 100,000 écus a year on his pets, and a baker was employed just to bake white bread loaves for them. When travelling to Lyon in 1586, he took 200 lapdogs. They were divided into groups of eight, and each group had their own governess, a female servant and a packhorse. When in Paris, Henri III confiscated dogs that caught his eye, even visiting nunneries to take those that he liked 'to the great regret and displeasure of the ladies who owned the dogs'. He gave the Order of the Holy Spirit, France's highest order of chivalry, to a man who gave him two Turqués dogs. In 1589 his current favourites, Liline, Titi and Mimi, slept on his bed. When Jacques Clément entered the royal presence disguised as a priest, Liline began barking furiously. Unfortunately her alarm was ignored and Clément fatally stabbed Henri.

———————◆———————

This seventeenth-century Florentine 'Portrait of a Dog' shows a quite contented fat little lapdog, complete with belled collar, sitting on a table with sweat treats to eat.

In 1751 the English novelist Francis Coventry wrote *The History of Pompey the Little, Or, the Life and Adventures of a Lap-Dog*, with thinly veiled references to contemporary society. Here, Pompey moves in with one Lady Tempest (undoubtedly Etheldreda, Viscountess Townshend (c.1708–1788)):

She returned home from her visit just as the clock was striking four, and after surveying herself a moment in the glass, and a little adjusting her hair, went directly to introduce master Pompey to his companions. These were an Italian grey-hound, a Dutch pug, two black spaniels of king Charles's breed, a harlequin grey-hound, a spotted Dane, and a mouse-colour'd English bull-dog. They heard their mistress's rap at the door, and were assembled in the dining-room, ready to receive her: But on the appearance of master Pompey, they set up a general bark, perhaps out of envy; and some of them treated the little stranger with rather more rudeness than was consistent with dogs of their education. However, the lady soon interposed her authority, and commanded silence among them, by ringing a little bell, which she kept by her for that purpose. They all obeyed the signal instantly, and were still in a moment; upon which she carried little Pompey round, and obliged them all to salute their new acquaintance, at the same time commanding some of them to ask pardon for their unpolite behaviour; which whether they understood or not, must be left to the reader's determination.

Pugs were introduced to the Netherlands from China in the sixteenth century, thanks to the Dutch East India Company. According to legend, William the Silent, Prince of Orange was woken by the barking of his pug Pompey during a midnight attack by the Spanish in 1572. He escaped in the nick of time, and from then on pugs became associated with the House of Orange. The breed became popular in England when William III brought a pug with him during the Glorious Revolution.

The Mops-Orden (the Order of the Pug) was a Catholic secret society founded in 1740 in Bavaria after Catholics were banned from joining the Freemasons. Initiates wore a dog collar and scratched the door, and were led around in circles while the members (Pugs of the Order) barked. It was banned in 1748.

Marie Antoinette, when travelling to France for her wedding, was parted from her pug Mops as he was thought be an unsuitable companion for the new French dauphine. Fortunately they were later reunited. On *Napoleon Bonaparte's* wedding night, he was bitten in bed by Josephine's pug Fortuné. The incident does not seem to have put Josephine off pugs, as she continued to keep them – they slept on cashmere shawls in her bedroom.

Oil painting of Princess Ekaterina Golitsyna with her pet pug, 1759.

The British poet Alexander Pope (1688-1744) kept a succession of Great Danes, all called Bounce. After receiving threats following the publication of *The Dunciad* in 1728, Pope would go out walking in Twickenham with two pistols and Bounce at his side. One of Bounce's puppies was presented at Kew Palace to Frederick, Prince of Wales, with following verse inscribed on its collar:

I am his Highness's dog at Kew
Pray tell me, sir, whose dog are you?

In 1744, shortly before his own death, Bounce died while in the care of the Earl of Orrery. Pope wrote a poem called 'Bounce to Pope' in which the dog waits in the afterlife for his master and addresses Pope:

So here I prick my ears and strain to mark
Thy slight form coming after through the dark
And leap to meet thee; with my deep bark drown
Thy: "Bounce! why Bounce, old friend! nay, down, Bounce, down!"

Portrait of Alexander Pope with Bounce, c.1718.

Frederick the Great, King of Prussia (reigned 1740-1786) adored his miniature greyhounds. They had their own quarters at Sans-Souci, where they would cheerfully rip up furniture to their owner's amusement, with his favourite one sleeping on the bed. When there was a fire at the palace he wrote that he managed to save 'his dog, jewels and books' and he wrote that he wished to buried with his dogs.

He was particularly fond of one called Biche, who even followed the king into battle, and when captured by Hungarian troops was repatriated back to Frederick after extensive negotiations. On her death Frederick wrote:

The faithfulness of this poor creature had so strongly attached me to her, her suffering so moved me, that, I confess, I am sad and afflicted. Does one have to be hard? Must one be insensitive? I believe that anyone capable of indifference towards a faithful animal is unable to be grateful towards an equal, and that, if one must choose, it is best to be too sensitive than too hard.

One of Frederick the Great's Italian greyhounds.

George Washington owned many dogs, mostly hounds. They included Sweet Lips, Truelove, Drunkard, Tipsy, Taster, Tipler, Ragman, and Vulcan. He also owned a coach dog named Madame Moose, purchased in 1786 for twelve shillings. A male coach dog was bought the following year, so that, as Washington recorded in his diary: 'A new coach dog [arrived] for the benefit of Madame Moose; her amorous fits should therefore be attended to.'

General Sir William Howe, Commander-in-Chief of British forces during the American War of Independence, lost his dog during the Battle of Germantown on 4 October 1777. With his owner's name inscribed on his collar tag, the dog had come with his master onto the field of battle – but left with the wrong army. General George Washington had the dog fed and cared for and it was returned to the British lines two days later with the following note, penned by his aide-de-camp:

General Washington's compliments to General Howe, does himself the pleasure to return him a Dog, which accidentally fell into his hands, and by the inscription on the Collar, appears to belong to General Howe.

In 1796 a *Dog Tax* was proposed in the British parliament by John Dent MP, in an attempt to raise funds to fight the war in France. It was argued and debated with great passion – its proponents insisted that pets were taxable luxuries, but for its opponents the bonds between dog and man should not be subject to taxation. They argued that the pet was a member of the household and the relationship between dog and master would turn from one of friendship to one of servitude.

Dent claimed that dogs ate a huge amount of food, thus limiting the country's supplies. The tax would make food cheaper, lessen the cases of hydrophobia (rabies) and raise a huge amount of revenue. Although his bill was defeated, within the month an act to tax dogs was introduced by Pitt the Younger's ministry. Unlike Dent's proposal, which had no exceptions, the new act tried to tax dogs kept as 'luxuries' and distinguished between the rich and poor. Owners of sporting dogs and those with two or more dogs were charged five shillings per dog. Those with only one non-working dog and already subject to window or house taxes would only owe three shillings. The tax stayed in place until 1882.

Detail from James Gillray's 'Questions & Commands' (1788).

Assorted poodles were involved in the *Napoleonic Wars*. in Russia, Sergeant Adrien Bourgogne met a man carrying a poodle called Mouton on his back, due to the dog's paws being frozen. Mouton had come from Spain and had travelled all over Europe with the regiment. Another poodle in the Russian campaign, Moffino, was separated from his Italian corporal in the chaos of crossing the Berezina river in 1812. It was claimed that Moffino walked all the way back to Italy, where he was reunited with his master.

Moustache, a black poodle, was the *regimental mascot* of French grenadiers, and took part in various military engagements. At Austerlitz, he dashed to the body of a young French ensign who was holding the regimental colours surrounded by the enemy and brought the colours back to his regiment. Another French poodle, Sancho, was adopted that same year at the battle of Salamanca by the Marquess of Worcester, who had found the dog lying on the grave of his master, a French lieutenant.

Munito the Wonderful Dog, owned by one Signor Castelli, was a famous performing poodle from the 1810s to the 1830s (there were probably at least two or three Munitos performing in Europe during this time). In the act, Munito apparently excelled at playing dominoes, doing sums and spelling out words in French, Italian and English using alphabet cards.

Charles Dickens claimed that he had discovered the secret when he noticed Munito sniffing the cards: 'a learned dog was exhibited in Piccadilly – Munito… He performed many curious feats, answering questions, telling the hour of the day… picking out any cards called for from a pack on the ground… [We] noticed that between each feat the master gave the dog some small bits… of food, and that there was a faint smell of aniseed from that corner of the room.'

For the author *Jules Verne* the trick lay in Munito's sense of sound – he asserted that Munito's owner snapped a toothpick in his pocket when the dog sniffed the correct card. Munito was a huge star all over Europe and America. Franz Lizst would complain that, as a concert pianist, he was just as dependent on the fickle public as Munito.

Mit Allerhöchster Bewilligung

wird

heute Montag den 1sten Dezember und die folgenden Tage

eine Abend-Unterhaltung

mit dem

nzig berühmten Hunde Munito

When the British poet *Lord Byron's beloved Newfoundland Boatswain* was infected with rabies, Byron nursed the dog before finally burying him in Newstead Abbey, with this poem on the dog's monument:

BOATSWAIN, a DOG,
who was born in Newfoundland May 1803,
and died at Newstead Nov. 18 1808....
But the poor Dog, in life the firmest friend,
The first to welcome, foremost to defend,
Whose honest heart is still his Master's own,
Who labours, fights, lives, breathes for him alone, ...
Ye, who behold perchance this simple urn,
Pass on – it honours none you wish to mourn.
To mark a friend's remains these stones arise;
I never knew but one -- and here he lies.

Plate 8

London: Pub.d May 26, 1797, by G.M. Woodward, Berners-Street.

Queen Victoria had a life-long attachment to dogs. Her first pet was Dash, a King Charles spaniel, a gift from her mother the Duchess of Kent in April 1833. That Christmas she gave him rubber balls and gingerbread as presents and referred to him in her diary as *'dear Dashy'* and 'dear sweet little Dash'. On the day of her coronation, 28 June 1838, Victoria raced up the stairs of Buckingham Palace after the ceremony to wash Dash, as it was his customary bath day.

When he died in December 1840 he was buried in the grounds of Windsor Castle with the epitaph:

Here lies
DASH
The favourite spaniel of Her Majesty Queen Victoria
In his 10th year
His attachment was without selfishness
His playfulness without malice
His fidelity without deceit
READER
If you would be beloved and die regretted
Profit by the example of
DASH

Sir Edwin Landseer's 1836 portrait of Queen Victoria's beloved dog Dash.

William Nicholson.

When Prince Albert came to Britain in 1840 to marry Queen Victoria, he brought his *greyhound Eos*, who was black with white patches. He had owned Eos since he was fourteen and described her as 'very friendly if there is plum-cake in the room... keen on hunting, sleepy after it, always proud and contemptuous of other dogs'.

Dachshunds were also introduced to the British royal family from Coburg, starting with Waldmann in 1840, and Deckel in 1845. The family owned a long succession of Waldmanns and Waldinas (Waldmann VI's memorial names him as 'the very favourite dachshund' of Queen Victoria). When Dacko died she wrote: 'I am greatly distressed at my dear old 'Dacko' having died. The dear old dog was so attached to me and had such funny amusing ways, with large melancholy expressive eyes, and was quite part of my daily life, always in my room, and I will miss him very much...' Victoria was also fond of smooth-haired collies, Skye terriers, pugs and Pomeranians – one of the latter sat on her death bed.

13

JULIA.

I should like to be "treated like a dog."

The poet *Elizabeth Barrett Browning* (1806-1861) wrote the poem 'To Flush, My Dog' to her beloved cocker spaniel:

LOVING friend, the gift of one,
Who, her own true faith, hath run,
Through thy lower nature;
Be my benediction said
With my hand upon thy head,
Gentle fellow-creature!

Like a lady's ringlets brown,
Flow thy silken ears adown
Either side demurely,
Of thy silver-suited breast
Shining out from all the rest
Of thy body purely.

… Blessings on thee, dog of mine,
Pretty collars make thee fine,
Sugared milk make fat thee!
Pleasures wag on in thy tail —
Hands of gentle motion fail
Nevermore, to pat thee!